ROOM FOR ME AND A MOUNTAIN LION

Here is a remarkable collection of tough, lean poems that speak in colloquial language of the joy and freedom in open spaces. Of the strangeness and danger of the natural world. Of nature as the last outpost against overcivilization. Of man as both alien and resident animal in a wondrous, threatened world. Over 100 poems selected—with the help of young readers who revel in what Whitman called "eating and sleeping with the earth"—by Nancy Larrick, author of **On City Streets.**

"This sensitive and well-selected collection of poems sings of a world that is becoming increasingly difficult to see as a reality . . . These poems set you dreaming. They may even send you back-packing." **—St. Louis Post-Dispatch**

"This collection . . . is one of the best of its kind—a joy to read and a delight to think of sharing." **—Kansas City Star**

Bantam Books by Nancy Larrick
Ask your bookseller for the books you missed

A PARENT'S GUIDE TO CHILDREN'S READING, Fourth Edition
ON CITY STREETS
ROOM FOR ME AND A MOUNTAIN LION

Room for Me and a Mountain Lion

Poetry of Open Space

Selected by Nancy Larrick

ILLUSTRATED WITH PHOTOGRAPHS

RLI | VLM 7 (VLR 3-8) / IL 6-adult

This low-priced Bantam Book has been completely reset in a type face designed for easy reading, and was printed from new plates. It contains the complete text of the original hard-cover edition.
NOT ONE WORD HAS BEEN OMITTED.

ROOM FOR ME AND A MOUNTAIN LION
A Bantam Book/published by arrangement with M. Evans and Company, Inc.

PRINTING HISTORY
M. Evans edition published July 1974
2nd printing September 1974
Bantam edition/October 1975

COPYRIGHT NOTICES AND ACKNOWLEDGMENTS
The copyright notices are listed below and on the pages following, which constitute an extension of this copyright page.

Thanks are due to the following authors, publishers, publications, and agents for permission to use the material included.

GEORGE ALLEN & UNWIN LTD. and HOUGHTON MIFFLIN COMPANY for "The Old Walking Song" from FELLOWSHIP OF THE RING by J. R. R. Tolkien. Copyright © 1966 by George Allen & Unwin Ltd. Reprinted by permission of the publishers.
ANTHENEUM PUBLISHERS, INC. for "Finding a Poem" by Eve Merriam from FINDING A POEM. Copyright © 1970 by Eve Merriam. Used by permission of Atheneum Publishers. Also for untitled Abanaki Indian song, untitled Eastern Eskimo song, and untitled Alaskan Eskimo song from SONGS OF THE DREAM PEOPLE; Chants and Images from the Indians and Eskimos of North America, edited by James Houston. (A Margaret K. McElderry Book) Copyright © 1972 by James Houston. Used with permission of Atheneum Publishers. Also for "German Shepherd" and "Grunion" by Myra Cohn Livingston, from THE MALIBU AND OTHER POEMS by Myra Cohn Livingston. (A Margaret K. McElderry Book) Text copyright © 1972 by Myra Cohn Livingston. Used by permission of Atheneum Publishers.
THE BODLEY HEAD and RANDOM HOUSE, INC. for "Zebra" from OUT OF AFRICA by Isak Dinesen. Copyright 1937 and renewed 1965 by Rungstedlundfonden. Reprinted by permission of Putnam, London and Random House, Inc.
THE CAXTON PRINTERS, LTD., Caldwell, Idaho for "The Cave" from Glenn Ward Dresbach's COLLECTED POEMS.
CHARLES M. CLEGG, JR. for the first and last stanzas of "Quid Restat" by Lucius M. Beebe, from CORYDON AND OTHER POEMS by Lucius M. Beebe. Copyright 1924 by B. J. Brimmer Company, Boston, Mass.
COWARD, McCANN & GEOGHEGAN, INC. for "West of Chicago" by John Dimoff from EARTH, AIR, FIRE AND WATER, edited by Frances Monson McCullough. Copyright © 1971 by Frances Monson McCullough. Reprinted by permission of Coward, McCann & Geoghegan, Inc.

0 9 8 7 6 5 4 3 2 1

CURTIS BROWN, LTD. for "Cicada" by Adrien Stoutenburg from HEROES ADVISE US, published by Charles Scribner's Sons, 1964. First published in *The New Yorker*. Copyright © 1964. Reprinted by permission of Curtis Brown, Ltd.
J. M. DENT & SONS LTD. and the Trustees for the Copyrights of the late Dylan Thomas and NEW DIRECTIONS PUBLISHING CORPORATION for an extract of 25 lines from UNDER MILK WOOD by Dylan Thomas. Copyright 1954 by New Directions Publishing Corporation. Reprinted by permission of the publishers.
THE DIAL PRESS/DELACORTE PRESS for "Morels" by William Jay Smith. Copyright © 1964 by William Jay Smith. Originally appeared in *The New Yorker*. Reprinted from the book NEW AND SELECTED POEMS by William Jay Smith with permission of the publisher. A Seymour Lawrence Book/ Delacorte Press.
DOUBLEDAY & COMPANY, INC. for "The Way through the Woods" copyright 1910 from RUDYARD KIPLING VERSE: Definitive Edition by Rudyard Kipling. Reprinted by permission of Mrs. George Bambridge and Doubleday & Company, Inc. Also for "Moss Gathering" copyright 1946 by Editorial Publications, Inc.; "Snake" copyright © 1955 by Theodore Roethke; "The Heron" copyright 1937 by Theodore Roethke; "The Waking" copyright 1948 by Theodore Roethke, from the book THE COLLECTED POEMS OF THEODORE ROETHKE. Reprinted by permission of Doubleday & Company, Inc.
FABER & FABER LTD. and HARPER & ROW, PUBLISHERS, INC. for "Bullfrog" from LUPERCAL by Ted Hughes. Copyright © 1959 by Ted Hughes. Originally appeared in *The New Yorker*. Reprinted by permission of the publishers.
THE GOLDEN QUILL PRESS and DANIEL SMYTHE for 3 lines from "Driftwood" by Daniel Smythe, published in the book GREEN DOORS by Daniel Smythe.
GRANADA PUBLISHING LIMITED for the extract "Alpine" from TARES by R. S. Thomas, published by Rupert Hart-Davis.
GROSSET & DUNLAP, INC. for "Who Am I?", reprinted from AT THE TOP OF MY VOICE AND OTHER POEMS by Felice Holman. Text copyright © 1970 by Felice Holman. Published by Grosset & Dunlap, Inc.
HARCOURT BRACE JOVANOVICH, INC. for "Summer Stars" and "Buffalo Dusk" from SMOKE AND STEEL by Carl Sandburg, copyright 1920, by Harcourt Brace Jovanovich, Inc.; renewed, 1948, by Carl Sandburg. Reprinted by permission of the publishers. Also for "Grassroots" from GOOD MORNING, AMERICA, copyright, 1928, 1956, by Carl Sandburg. Reprinted by permission of Harcourt Brace Jovanovich, Inc. Also for "Improved Farm Land from SLABS OF THE SUNBURNT WEST by Carl Sandburg, copyright, 1922, by Harcourt Brace Jovanovich, Inc.; renewed, 1950, by Carl Sandburg. Reprinted by permission of the publishers. Also for "To Look at Any Thing," © 1961 by John Moffitt. Reprinted from his volume THE LIVING SEED by permission of Harcourt Brace Jovanovich, Inc.
HARPER & ROW, PUBLISHERS, INC. for "In A Mountain Cabin in Norway" from SLEEPERS JOINING HANDS by Robert Bly. Copyright © 1973 by Robert Bly. Also for "May 10th"—Copyright © 1964 by Maxine Kumin, originally published in *The New Yorker*, and "The Hermit Picks Berries"—Copyright © 1972 by Maxine Kumin, from UP COUNTRY by Maxine Kumin. Also for "The Presence"—Copyright © 1969 by Maxine Kumin and "Riding in The Rain"—Copyright © 1970 by Maxine Kumin, from THE NIGHTMARE FACTORY by Maxine Kumin. Also for "Listening" from THE RESCUED YEAR by William Stafford. Copyright © 1960 by William E. Stafford; for "A Story" —Copyright © 1966 by William Stafford, "Behind the Falls," "With Kit, Age 7, at the Beach" (1966), "A Sound from the Earth"—Copyright © 1967 by William Stafford, "In Fur"—Copyright © 1967 by William Stafford, "Father's Voice"—Copyright © 1967 by William Stafford, and "Stories from Kansas" (1968) from ALLEGIANCES by William Stafford. Also for "Late at Night"—Copyright 1954 by William Stafford, "Holding the Sky"—Copyright © 1957 by William Stafford, "Found in a Storm"—Copyright © 1961 by William Stafford, and "The View from Here"—Copyright © 1962 by William Stafford, from TRAVELING THROUGH THE DARK by William Stafford. Reprinted by permission of Harper & Row, Publishers, Inc.
HOLT, RINEHART AND WINSTON, INC. for "The Road Not Taken," "Sand Dunes," "An Empty Threat," and "Blue-Butterfly Day" from THE POETRY OF ROBERT FROST edited by Edward Connery Lathem. Copyright 1916, 1923, 1928, © 1969 by Holt, Rinehart and Winston, Inc. Copyright 1944, 1951, © 1956 by Robert Frost. Reprinted by permission of Holt, Rinehart and Winston, Inc.

HOUGHTON MIFFLIN COMPANY for "On Hardscrabble Mountain," "In Fields of Summer," and "Ruins Under the Stars" from Galway Kinnell's FLOWER HERDING ON MOUNT MONADNOCK. Copyright © 1964 by Galway Kinnell. Reprinted by permission of Houghton Mifflin Company. Also for "To Christ, Our Lord" from Galway Kinnell. Reprinted by permission of Houghton Mifflin Company. Also for "The Bear" from Galway Kinnell's BODY RAGS. Copyright © 1967 by Galway Kinnell. Reprinted by permission of Houghton Mifflin Company.
INDIANA UNIVERSITY PRESS for "Staying Alive" from STAYING ALIVE by David Wagoner, published by Indiana University Press.
LITTLE, BROWN AND COMPANY for "Crows" from FAR AND FEW by David McCord, by permission of Little, Brown and Company.
LONGMAN CANADA LTD. for an untitled Abanaki song, an untitled Eastern Eskimo song, and an untitled Alaskan Eskimo song, from SONGS OF THE DREAM PEOPLE: CHANTS AND IMAGES FROM THE INDIANS AND ESKIMOS OF NORTH AMERICA, edited by James Houston. Copyright © 1972 by James Houston.
MACMILLAN PUBLISHING CO., INC. for "Bats," "The Bird of Night," and "The Mockingbird" (originally appeared in *The New Yorker*). Reprinted with permission of Macmillan Publishing Co., Inc. from THE BAT-POET by Randall Jarrell. Copyright © by Macmillan Publishing Co., Inc. 1963, 1964. Also for "Storm Tides on Mejit." Reprinted with permission of Macmillan Publishing Co., Inc. from THE UNWRITTEN SONG, VOLUME 2, edited and with translations by Willard R. Trask. Copyright © 1967 by Willard R. Trask. Also for "An Indian Summer Day on the Prairie." Reprinted with permission of Macmillan Publishing Co., Inc. from COLLECTED POEMS by Vachel Lindsay. Copyright 1914 by Macmillan Publishing Co., Inc., renewed 1942 by Elizabeth C. Lindsay.
McINTOSH AND OTIS, INC. for "Mill Valley." Copyright © 1969 by Myra Cohn Livingston. From A CRAZY FLIGHT AND OTHER POEMS. Reprinted by permission of McIntosh and Otis, Inc.
THE MODERN POETRY ASSOCIATION for "Deer Hunt" by Judson Jerome, which first appeared in *Poetry*, copyright © 1955 by The Modern Poetry Association. Reprinted by permission of the Editor of *Poetry*.
WILLIAM MORROW & CO., INC. for "Swallows" by Thomas Hornsby Ferril. Reprinted by permission of William Morrow & Co., Inc. from WORDS FOR DENVER AND OTHER POEMS by Thomas Hornsby Ferril. Copyright © 1964, 1966 by Thomas Hornsby Ferril.
NEW DIRECTIONS PUBLISHING CORPORATION for "The Resolve" and "The Breathing" from Denise Levertov, O TASTE AND SEE. Copyright © 1964 by Denise Levertov Goodman. "The Breathing" was first published in *Poetry in Crystal*. Copyright © 1963 by Steuben Glass. Reprinted by permission of New Directions Publishing Corporation. Also for "Half Moon," translated by W. S. Mervin, from Federico Garcia Lorca, SELECTED POEMS. Copyright 1955 by New Directions Publishing Corporation. Reprinted by permission of New Directions Publishing Corporation.
THE NEW YORKER and WILLIAM STAFFORD for "Moles" by William Stafford. Reprinted by permission; © 1950 The New Yorker Magazine, Inc.
PRENTICE-HALL INC. for "The Flower-Fed Buffaloes" from GOING TO THE STARS by Vachel Lindsay, copyright 1926 by D. Appleton and Company. Reprinted by permission of Prentice-Hall Inc.
G. P. PUTNAM'S SONS for "When Spring Came" (Tlingit song) from THE TURQUOISE HORSE by Flora Hood. Copyright © 1972 by Flora Hood. Reprinted by permission of G. P. Putnam's Sons.
QUARTERLY REVIEW OF LITERATURE for "A Campfire and Ants" by Alexander Solzhenitsyn. Reprinted from *Quarterly Review of Literature*, Volume XVII, # 1/2.
RANDOM HOUSE, INC./ALFRED A. KNOPF, INC. for "Earthy Anecdote." Copyright 1923 and renewed 1951 by Wallace Stevens. Reprinted from THE COLLECTED POEMS OF WALLACE STEVENS by permission of Alfred A. Knopf, Inc. Also for seven lines from "My First Summer in the Sierra" by John Muir, from THE MOUNTAINS AND THE SHORE, A PORTFOLIO CALENDAR, by Richard Kauffman.
ROUTLEDGE & KEGAN PAUL LTD. for "April" from COLLECTED POEMS by Yvor Winters.
ALMA J. SARETT for "Four Little Foxes" by Lew Sarett. From COVENANT WITH EARTH: A SELECTION FROM THE POEMS OF LEW SARETT. Edited, 1956, by Alma Johnson Sarett. Gainesville: University of Florida Press, 1956. Reprinted by permission of Mrs. Sarett.

CHARLES SCRIBNER'S SONS for permission to reprint the following poems by May Swenson from ICONOGRAPHS: "A Pair" (Copyright © 1970 May Swenson), "How Everything Happens" (Copyright © 1969 May Swenson), and "Beginning to Squall" (Copyright © 1968 May Swenson). Also for "The Woods at Night" from TO MIX WITH TIME by May Swenson. Copyright © 1963 May Swenson. Also for "Nebraska" from POETS OF TODAY VII: JOURNEYS AND RETURN: POEMS by Jon Swan. Copyright © 1960 Jon Swan.
WILLIAM JAY SMITH for "Seal." Copyright © 1957 by William Jay Smith. Reprinted by permission of William Jay Smith.
STANFORD UNIVERSITY PRESS for "The Hermit" by Hsü Pên. Reprinted from POEMS OF THE HUNDRED NAMES by Henry H. Hart with the permission of the publishers, Stanford University Press. Copyright 1933, 1938 by the Regents of the University of California. Copyright 1954 by the Board of Trustees of the Leland Stanford Junior University.
MAY SWENSON for permission to reprint "Waking from a Nap on the Beach" and "Out of the Sea, Early." Copyright © by May Swenson 1967 in the collection HALF SUN HALF SLEEP.
THE UNIVERSITY OF MASSACHUSETTS PRESS for "Skier" and "Seagulls" by Robert Francis. Reprinted by permission of Robert Francis and The University of Massachusetts Press from COME OUT INTO THE SUN: NEW AND SELECTED POEMS by Robert Francis, © Copyright, 1965.
THE VIKING PRESS, INC. for "Mountain Lion" and "A Living" from THE COMPLETE POEMS OF D. H. LAWRENCE edited by Vivian de Sola Pinto and F. Warren Roberts. Copyright © 1964, 1971 by Angelo Ravagli and C. M. Weekley, Executors of the Estate of Frieda Lawrence Ravagli. All rights reserved. Reprinted by permission of the Viking Press, Inc.
A. P. WATT & SON for "The Way through the Woods," from REWARDS AND FAIRIES by Rudyard Kipling. Reprinted by permission of Mrs. George Bambridge and Macmillan Co. of Canada.
WESLEYAN UNIVERSITY PRESS for "Here in Katmandu" by Donald Justice. Copyright © 1956 by Donald Justice. Reprinted from THE SUMMER ANNIVERSARIES, by Donald Justice, by permission of Wesleyan University Press. "Here in Katmandu" first appeared in *Poetry*.
THE WILDERNESS SOCIETY for "Requiem for a River" by Kim Williams and "Hard Questions" by Margaret Tsuda. Reprinted from *The Living Wilderness*, by permission.
NANCY WOODS for "I Read a Tight-Fisted Poem Once." Reprinted by permission of the author.
THE WORLD PUBLISHING COMPANY for "Eskimo Chant." Reprinted by permission of The World Publishing Company from BEYOND THE HILLS: A BOOK OF ESKIMO POEMS by Knud Rasmussen. Copyright © 1961 by The World Publishing Company.
AL YOUNG for "For Poets." Copyright © 1968 by Al Young. Reprinted by permission of the author.

PICTURE CREDITS

Title page and pages 6, 16, 26, 29, 39, 44, 48, 53, 66, 68, 75, 77, 80, 82, 88, 93, 94, 101, 108, 119, 123, 127, 133, 135, 142, and 147 by Stephen B. Nichols.
Page xvi, photo by Wilford L. Miller from National Audubon Society.
Page 15, photo by Dan Guravich from Photo Researchers.
Pages 50 and 51, photo by Diana Bryant.
Page 61, photo by Joe van Wormer from Photo Researchers.
Page 96, photo by Howard Cleaves from National Audubon Society.

Published simultaneously in the United States and Canada

Bantam Books are published by Bantam Books, Inc. Its trademark, consisting of the words "Bantam Books" and the portrayal of a bantam, is registered in the United States Patent Office and in other countries. Marca Registrada. Bantam Books, Inc., 666 Fifth Avenue, New York, New York 10019.

PRINTED IN THE UNITED STATES OF AMERICA

For Alec Crosby
who introduced me
to trapdoor spiders,
bottle gentians,
and ringing rocks.

CONTENTS

ROOM FOR ME AND A MOUNTAIN LION

My first adventure in the wilderness was in New Mexico, where my husband and I spent ten days exploring the Pecos Wilderness on horseback. It was late September and cold enough one night to encrust our tent ropes with ice and dust the ground with snow. But by noon the air was warm and the sun on the shimmering aspen leaves made a canopy of gold.

From the overlook the wranglers pointed out elk and bighorn sheep across the ravine, and once I saw the white rump of a mule deer skittering through an open meadow to shelter in the woods beyond.

"We *could* see a mountain lion," said Wes Adams, the head wrangler, "but most likely we won't. They're getting scarcer every year." We never did see a mountain lion.

But some years later, in a poem by D. H. Lawrence, I met a mountain lion I shall never forget. He was a gorgeous creature hanging lifeless across the shoulder of a hunter coming out of Lobo Canyon in New Mexico. With the poet I found myself retracing our old horseback trail in the Pecos Wilderness. Now I was doubly sure that there must be "room for me and a mountain lion," as Lawrence put it.

A horseback trip has its special glory, but to move into harmony with the wilderness, there is nothing like backpacking. Steadily you push on, carrying everything you need to survive, and at the same time seeing details of rocks and plants and wildlife no horseback rider can possibly take in.

We had that experience in Baja California, where we backpacked from towering ponderosa pine country a mile high, down through the Lost Canyon of Cantil, to the open desert almost five days beyond. The first night we camped on a broad ledge halfway down to the canyon floor, hoarding each drop of water we carried until we could reach the stream below. A rugged way to spend a vacation! But the Easter sunrise seen from our rocky perch was beyond belief, and the radiance it cast on the sheer rock face of the mountain beside us was breathtaking.

A few days later we were swimming in a pool formed by the tiny canyon stream. Sprays of miniature orchids leaned toward the water, and the rare blue palms, drooping with cascades of dates, stood guard. Next day the stream had vanished, and we were in open desert.

I am not sure that Whitman had such a trail as this in mind when he said, "Afoot and light-hearted I take to the open road." But I think ours gave us the same feeling of light-heartedness and freedom that he described in 1855 in his poem "Song of the Open Road."

Whitman was 35 then, bold of spirit and determined to be himself in a world trying to ram him into its mold. In that day America was largely rural, and for Whitman the open road was "a long brown path."

Today the open road is a six-lane highway, defaced with billboards and beer cans. Open space is vanishing, but our need for freedom to breathe pure air, climb rocky trails, and observe the tiniest creatures persists. Backpackers push across alpine plateaus and on to high tundra above the timberline. Canoeists run the rapids to reach a choice camp site.

From a sleeping bag on high open ground, you get a fresh view of the world. I shall never forget the night hawks wheeling and plunging above us on a broad plateau above the Missouri River, which we had been exploring by raft. Or the pink sunrise glow spreading across the desert into Lost Canyon.

Whether such experiences make a poet or whether the poet seeks them out I do not know. But the fact is that many poets—particularly our modern poets—have turned from the brutal turmoil of urban living to explore rocky trails or follow animal tracks across the snow. Like Eve Merriam, they go "where there seems no way to go"—and find a poem.

ROOM FOR ME AND A MOUNTAIN LION is a collection of these poems of open space. They have been selected with the help of young readers who revel in what Whitman calls, "eating and sleeping with the earth."

NANCY LARRICK

Quakertown, Pennsylvania
November 1, 1973

High on
the Mountainside

MOUNTAIN LION

Climbing through the January snow, into the Lobo
    Canyon
Dark grow the spruce-trees, blue is the balsam, water
    sounds still unfrozen, and the trail is evident.

Men!
Two men!
Men! The only animal in the world to fear!

They hesitate.
We hesitate.
They have a gun.
We have no gun.

Then we all advance, to meet.

Two Mexicans, strangers, emerging out of the dark and
    snow and inwardness of the Lobo valley.
What are they doing here on this vanishing trail?

What is he carrying?
Something yellow.
A deer?

Qué tiene, amigo?
León—

He smiles, foolishly, as if he were caught doing wrong.
And we smile, foolishly, as if we didn't know.
He is quite gentle and dark-faced.

It is a mountain lion,
A long, long slim cat, yellow like a lioness.
Dead.

He trapped her this morning, he says, smiling foolishly.

Lift up her face,
Her round, bright face, bright as frost.
Her round, fine-fashioned head, with two dead ears;
And stripes in the brilliant frost of her face, sharp, fine
dark rays,
Dark, keen, fine rays in the brilliant frost of her face.
Beautiful dead eyes.

Hermoso es!

They go out towards the open;
We go on into the gloom of Lobo.

And above the trees I found her lair,
A hole in the blood-orange brilliant rocks that stick up,
a little cave.
And bones, and twigs, and a perilous ascent.

So, she will never leap up that way again, with the
yellow flash of a mountain lion's long shoot!
And her bright striped frost-face will never watch any
more, out of the shadow of the cave in the blood-
orange rock,
Above the trees of the Lobo dark valley-mouth!

Instead, I look out.
And out to the dim of the desert, like a dream, never
    real;
To the snow of the Sangre de Cristo mountains, the ice
    of the mountains of Picoris,
And near across the opposite steep of snow, green trees
    motionless standing in snow, like a Christmas toy.

And I think in this empty world there was room for me
    and a mountain lion.
And I think in the world beyond, how easily we might
    spare a million or two of humans
And never miss them.
Yet what a gap in the world, the missing white frost-face
    of that slim yellow mountain lion!

D. H. LAWRENCE

IN A MOUNTAIN CABIN IN NORWAY

I look down the mountainside. Just below my window
several grasses growing raggedly together.

The noise of the snowfed river
winds into the ear, far back into the head.
At three A.M. the big peaks are still lit.

I look over to the other mountainside.
So many pines the eye can't count them!
Sparks of darkness float around me.
No one comes to visit us for a week.

ROBERT BLY

FINDING A POEM

1

Trail climbing
you have to watch your footing
tricky with fallen rocks and mosses that crumble
leafmold slippery
hold onto a bush
it springs back
scratching your face
your heart is pounding
your legs are ready to cave in
why do mountains have to be so steep
can't they put them in the plain

you can barely discern the ferns and laurel
amid the tangled brush
the evergreens *are* majestic but
sweating you've rubbed a blister
bugs to slap away
a dried-out stream bed
stony stony
until abruptly
light dazzling
you're in the clear
the air is the highest note ever sung
listen you can hear it echoing

all the way down
while here you kingly are
crowning the world
with this view that
is impossible to describe
a poem.

2

Where there seems no way to go
go anyway
don't be put off by what you can't see
get up any which way
scramble on hands and knees
ditching your pride
slide along the bottom for a stretch
clutch at roots
and keep going on

once up there you can look back to
the pathway you have cleared
that will make it easier
next time you climb.

3

Climbing often
not just for the music
but for the in between
the lights and darks of greenery
the patterns of touch
make it a ritual
of going round the same trees
sitting on the same lichen benches
pausing for second breath at the same log
a tradition by now
and yet
you can never duplicate the climb
every time is the first anew.

EVE MERRIAM

ON HARDSCRABBLE MOUNTAIN

1

On old slashed spruce boughs
Buoying me off the snow
I stretched out on the mountain,
Now and then a bit of snow
Would glide quietly from a branch,

Once a last deerfly came by,

I could see off for about a hundred miles.

2

I waked with a start,
The sun had crawled off me,
I was shivering in thick blue shadows,
Sap had stuck me to the spruce boughs,

Far away I could hear
The wind starting to rise.

3

On the way down, passing
The little graveyard in the woods,
I gave a thought to the old skulls and bones lying there,
And I started praying to a bear just shutting his eyes,
To a skunk dozing off,
To a marmot with yellow belly,
To a dog-faced hedgehog,
To a dormouse with a paunch and large cars like leaves
or wings.

GALWAY KINNELL

A STORY

After they passed I climbed
out of my hole and sat
in the sun again. Loose rocks
all around make it safe—I can
hear anyone moving. It often
troubles me to think how others
dare live where stealth is possible,
and how they can feel safe, considering
all the narrow places,
without whiskers.

Anyway, those climbers were a puzzle—
above where I live nothing lives.
And they never came down. There is no
other way. The way it is,
they crawl far before they die.
I make my hole the deepest one
this high on the mountainside.

WILLIAM STAFFORD

SKIER

He swings down like the flourish of a pen
Signing a signature in white on white.

The silence of his skis reciprocates
The silence of the world around him.

Wind is his one competitor
In the cool winding and unwinding down.

On incandescent feet he falls
Unfalling, trailing white foam, white fire.

ROBERT FRANCIS

DEER HUNT

Because the warden is a cousin, my
mountain friends hunt in summer when the deer
cherish each rattler-ridden spring, and I
have waited hours by a pool in fear
that manhood would require I shoot or that
the steady drip of the hill would dull my ear
to a snake whispering near the log I sat
upon, and listened to the yelping cheer
of dogs and men resounding ridge to ridge.
I flinched at every lonely rifle crack,
my knuckles whitening where I gripped the edge
of age and clung, like retching, sinking back,
then gripping once again the monstrous gun—
since I, to be a man, had taken one.

JUDSON JEROME

THE CAVE

Sometimes when the boy was troubled he would go
 To a little cave of stone above the brook
And build a fire just big enough to glow
 Upon the ledge outside, then sit and look.
Below him was the winding silver trail
 Of water from the upland pasture springs,
And meadows where he heard the calling quail;
 Before him was the sky, and passing wings.

The tang of willow twigs he lighted there,
 Fragrance of meadows breathing slow and deep,
The cave's own musky coolness on the air,
 The scent of sunlight . . . all were his to keep.
We had such places—cave or tree or hill . . .
 And we are lucky if we keep them still.

GLENN W. DRESBACH

FOUND IN A STORM

A storm that needed a mountain
met it where we were:
we woke up in a gale
that was reasoning with our tent,
and all the persuaded snow
streaked along, guessing the ground.

We turned from that curtain, down.
But sometime we will turn
back to the curtain and go
by plan through an unplanned storm,
disappearing into the cold,
meanings in search of a world.

WILLIAM STAFFORD

HOLDING THE SKY

We saw a town by the track in Colorado.
Cedar trees below had sifted the air,
snow water foamed the torn river there,
and a lost road went climbing the slope like a ladder.

We were traveling between a mountain and Thursday,
holding pages back on the calendar,
remembering every turn in the roadway:
we could hold that sky, we said, and remember.

On the western slope we crashed into Thursday.
"So long," you said when the train stopped there.
Snow was falling, touching in the air.
Those dark mountains have never wavered.

WILLIAM STAFFORD

HERE IN KATMANDU

We have climbed the mountain
There's nothing more to do.
It is terrible to come down
To the valley
Where, amidst many flowers,
One thinks of snow.

As formerly, amidst snow,
Climbing the mountain,

One thought of flowers,
Tremulous, ruddy with dew,
In the valley.
One caught their scent coming down.

It is difficult to adjust, once down,
To the absence of snow.
Clear days, from the valley,
One looks up at the mountain.
What else is there to do?
Prayerwheels, flowers!

Let the flowers
Fade, the prayerwheels run down.
What have these to do
With us who have stood atop the snow
Atop the mountain,
Flags seen from the valley?

It might be possible to live in the valley,
To bury oneself among flowers,
If one could forget the mountain,
How, setting out before dawn,
Blinded with snow,
One knew what to do.

Meanwhile it is not easy here in Katmandu,
Especially when to the valley
That wind which means snow
Elsewhere, but here means flowers,
Comes down,
As soon it must, from the mountain.

DONALD JUSTICE

REQUIEM FOR A RIVER

"So we diverted the river," he said,
showing blueprints
and maps
and geological surveys.
"It'll go in this canal now."

The Rio Blanco River starts in a glacier
up the white-capped Andes.
It has run through a green valley
for three million years,
maybe more.

Now in this year
when the Rio Blanco copper mine
at 12,000 feet altitude
gets underway,
the river has to go.

Pick it up,
Move it over—
Anything is possible.
Don't stand in the way
of progress,
And a 90-million-dollar mine.
"We concreted the dam," Bert said.

Thanks.

KIM WILLIAMS

ALPINE

About mountains it is useless to argue,
You have either been up or you haven't;

The view from halfway is nobody's view.
The best flowers are mostly at the top

Under a ledge, nourished by the wind.
A sense of smell is of less importance

Than a sense of balance, walking on clouds
Through holes in which you can see the earth

Like a rich man through the eye of a needle.
The mind has its own level to find.

R. S. THOMAS

From garden to garden, ridge to ridge,
I drifted enchanted . . .
gazing afar over domes and peaks, lakes and woods,
and the billowy glaciated fields . . .
In the midst of such beauty, pierced with its rays,
one's body is all one tingling palate.
Who wouldn't be a mountaineer!

JOHN MUIR

Through the Woods

THE WAY THROUGH THE WOODS

They shut the road through the woods
Seventy years ago.
Weather and rain have undone it again,
And now you would never know
There was once a road through the woods
Before they planted the trees.
It is underneath the coppice and heath
And the thin anemones.
Only the keeper sees
That, where the ring-dove broods,
And the badgers roll at ease,
There was once a road through the woods.

Yet, if you enter the woods
Of a summer evening late,
When the night-air cools on the trout-ringed pools
Where the otter whistles his mate,
(They fear not men in the woods,
Because they see so few.)
You will hear the beat of a horse's feet,
And the swish of a skirt in the dew,
Steadily cantering through
The misty solitudes,
As though they perfectly knew
The old lost road through the woods. . . .

But there is no road through the woods.

RUDYARD KIPLING

THE ROAD NOT TAKEN

Two roads diverged in a yellow wood,
And sorry I could not travel both
And be one traveler, long I stood
And looked down one as far as I could
To where it bent in the undergrowth;

Then took the other, as just as fair,
And having perhaps the better claim,
Because it was grassy and wanted wear;
Though as for that, the passing there
Had worn them really about the same,

And both that morning equally lay
In leaves no step had trodden black.
Oh, I kept the first for another day!
Yet knowing how way leads on to way,
I doubted if I should ever come back.

I shall be telling this with a sigh
Somewhere ages and ages hence:
Two roads diverged in a wood, and I—
I took the one less traveled by,
And that has made all the difference.

ROBERT FROST

MOSS-GATHERING

To loosen with all ten fingers held wide and limber
And lift up a patch, dark-green, the kind for lining
cemetery baskets,
Thick and cushiony, like an old-fashioned doormat,
The crumbling small hollow sticks on the underside
mixed with roots,
And wintergreen berries and leaves still stuck to the
top,—
That was moss-gathering.
But something always went out of me when I dug loose
those carpets
Of green, or plunged to my elbows in the spongy yel-
lowish moss of the marshes:
And afterwards I always felt mean, jogging back over
the logging road,
As if I had broken the natural order of things in that
swampland;
Disturbed some rhythm, old and of vast importance,
By pulling off flesh from the living planet;
As if I had committed, against the whole scheme of life,
a desecration.

THEODORE ROETHKE

MORELS

A wet gray day—rain falling slowly, mist over the valley, mountains dark circumflex smudges in the distance—

Apple blossoms just gone by, the branches feathery still as if fluttering with half-visible antennae—

A day in May like so many in these green mountains, and I went out just as I had last year

At the same time, and found them there under the big maples—by the bend in the road—right where they had stood

Last year and the year before that, risen from the dark duff of the woods, emerging at odd angles

From spores hidden by curled and matted leaves, a fringe of rain on the grass around them,

Beads of rain on the mounded leaves and mosses round them,

Not in a ring themselves but ringed by jack-in-the-pulpits with deep eggplant-colored stripes;

Not ringed but rare, not gilled but polyp-like, having sprung up overnight—

These mushrooms of the gods, resembling human organs uprooted, rooted only on the air,

Looking like lungs wrenched from the human body, lungs reversed, not breathing internally

But being the externalization of breath itself, these spicy, twisted cones,

These perforated brown-white asparagus tips—these morels, smelling of wet graham crackers mixed with maple leaves;

And, reaching down by the pale green fern shoots, I nipped their pulpy stems at the base

And dropped them into a paper bag—a damp brown bag (their color)—and carried

Them (weighing absolutely nothing) down the hill and into the house; you held them

Under cold bubbling water and sliced them with a surgeon's stroke clean through,

And sautéed them over a low flame, butter-brown; and
we ate them then and there—

Tasting of the sweet damp woods and of the rain one
inch above the meadow:

It was like feasting upon air.

WILLIAM JAY SMITH

FOUR LITTLE FOXES

Speak gently, Spring, and make no sudden sound;
For in my windy valley, yesterday I found
Newborn foxes squirming on the ground—
        Speak gently.

Walk softly, March, forbear the bitter blow;
Her feet within a trap, her blood upon the snow,
The four little foxes saw their mother go—
        Walk softly.

Go lightly, Spring, oh, give them no alarm;
When I covered them with boughs to shelter them from
        harm
The thin blue foxes suckled at my arm—
        Go lightly.

Step softly, March, with your rampant hurricane;
Nuzzling one another, and whimpering with pain,
The new little foxes are shivering in the rain—
    Step softly.

LEW SARETT

A CAMPFIRE AND ANTS

I threw a small rotten log onto the fire, didn't examine it closely to see that its insides were thickly settled with ants.

The log began to crackle; ants tumbled out and ran off in despair. They ran along the top and writhed, burning in the flames. I grabbed the log and rolled it aside. Now many of the ants escaped—they ran down to the sand, to the pine needles.

But what was strange: they didn't run away from the fire.

Barely having overcome their terror, they turned, swung around, and—some sort of power drew them back, to the abandoned home!—and there were many of these who again ran onto the burning log, rushed along it and perished there.

ALEXANDER SOLZHENITSYN

THE BIRD OF NIGHT

A shadow is floating through the moonlight.
Its wings don't make a sound.
Its claws are long, its beak is bright.
Its eyes try all the corners of the night.

It calls and calls: all the air swells and heaves
And washes up and down like water.
The ear that listens to the owl believes
In death. The bat beneath the eaves,

The mouse beside the stone are still as death.
The owl's air washes them like water.
The owl goes back and forth inside the night,
And the night holds its breath.

RANDALL JARRELL

THE RESOLVE

To come to the river
the brook
hurtles through rainy
woods, over-
topping rocks that
before the rain were
islands.

Its clearness
is gone, and
the song.
It is a rich brown, a load
of churned earth
goes with it.

The sound now
is a direct, intense
sound of
direction.

DENISE LEVERTOV

A PAIR

A he
and she,
prowed upstream,
soot-brown
necks,
bills the green
of spring
asparagus,

heads
proud figure-
heads for the boat-
bodies, smooth
hulls on feathered
water,

the two,
browed with light,
steer ashore,
rise; four
web-
paddles pigeon-
toe it
to the reeds;

he
walks first,
proud, prowed
as when light-
browed, swimming,
he leads.

MAY SWENSON

BEHIND THE FALLS

First the falls, then the cave:
then sheets of sound around us fell
while earth fled inward, where we went.
We traced it back, cigarette lighter high—
lost the roof, then the wall,
found abruptly in that space
only the flame and ourselves,
and heard the curtain like the earth
go down, so still it made the lighter
dim that led us on under the hill.

We stopped, afraid—lost
if ever that flame went out—
and surfaced in each other's eyes,
two real people suddenly
more immediate in the dark
than in the sun we'd ever be.
When men and women meet that way
the curtain of the earth descends, and they
find how faint the light has been, how far
mere honesty or justice is from all they need.

WILLIAM STAFFORD

STAYING ALIVE

Staying alive in the woods is a matter of calming down
At first and deciding whether to wait for rescue,
Trusting to others,
Or simply to start walking and walking in one direction
Till you come out—or something happens to stop you.
By far the safer choice
Is to settle down where you are, and try to make a living
Off the land, camping near water, away from shadows.
Eat no white berries;
Spit out all bitterness. Shooting at anything
Means hiking further and further every day
To hunt survivors;
It may be best to learn what you have to learn without
    a gun,
Not killing but watching birds and animals go
In and out of shelter
At will. Following their example, build for a whole
    season:
Facing across the wind to your lean-to,
You may feel wilder,
And nothing, not even you, will have to stay in hiding.
If you have no matches, a stick and a fire-bow

Will keep you warmer,
Or the crystal of your watch, filled with water, held up
to the sun
Will do the same, in time. In case of snow,
Drifting toward winter,
Don't try to stay awake through the night, afraid of
freezing—
The bottom of your mind knows all about zero;
It will turn you over
And shake you till you waken. If you have trouble
sleeping
Even in the best of weather, jumping to follow
The unidentifiable noises of the night and feeling
Bears and packs of wolves nuzzling your elbow,
Remember the trappers
Who treated them indifferently and were left alone.
If you hurt yourself, no one will comfort you
Or take your temperature,
So stumbling, wading, and climbing are as dangerous as
flying.
But if you decide, at last, you must break through
In spite of all danger,
Think of yourself by time and not by distance,
counting
Wherever you're going by how long it takes you;
No other measure
Will bring you safe to nightfall. Follow no streams:
they run
Under the ground or fall into wilder country.

Remember the stars
And moss when your mind runs into circles. If it should
rain,
Or the fog should roll the horizon in around you,
Hold still for hours
Or days, if you must, or weeks, for seeing is believing
In the wilderness. And if you find a pathway,
Wheel rut, or fence wire,
Retrace it left or right—someone knew where he was
going
Once upon a time, and you can follow
Hopefully, somewhere,
Just in case. There may even come, on some uncanny
evening,
A time when you're warm and dry, well fed, not thirsty,
Uninjured, without fear,
When nothing, either good or bad, is happening.
This is called staying alive. It's temporary.
What occurs after
Is doubtful. You must always be ready for something
to come bursting
Through the far edge of a clearing, running toward you,
Grinning from ear to ear
And hoarse with welcome. Or something crossing and
hovering

Overhead, as light as air, like a break in the sky,
Wondering what you are.
Here you are face to face with the problem of
recognition.
Having no time to make smoke, too much to say,
You should have a mirror
With a tiny hole in the back for better aiming, for
reflecting
Whatever disaster you can think of, to show
The way you suffer.
These body signals have universal meaning: If you are
lying
Flat on your back with arms outstretched behind you,
You say you require
Emergency treatment, if you are standing erect and
holding
Arms horizontal, you mean you are not ready;
If you hold them over
Your head, you want to be picked up. Three of anything
Is a sign of distress. Afterward, if you see
No ropes, no ladders,
No maps or messages falling, no searchlights or trails
blazing,
Then chances are, you should be prepared to burrow
Deep for a deep winter.

DAVID WAGONER

On the Prairies

from

NIGHT ON THE PRAIRIES

Night on the prairies,
The supper is over, the fire on the ground burns low,
The wearied emigrants sleep, wrapt in their blankets;
I walk by myself—I stand and look at the stars, which
I think now I never realized before.

WALT WHITMAN

SUMMER STARS

Bend low again, night of summer stars.
So near you are, sky of summer stars,
So near, a long arm man can pick off stars,
Pick off what he wants in the sky bowl,
So near you are, summer stars,
So near, strumming, strumming,
So lazy and hum-strumming.

CARL SANDBURG

AN INDIAN SUMMER DAY ON THE PRAIRIE

In the Beginning
The sun is a huntress young,
The sun is a red, red joy,
The sun is an Indian girl,
Of the tribe of the Illinois.

Mid-Morning
The sun is a smoldering fire,
That creeps through the high gray plain,
And leaves not a bush of cloud
To blossom with flowers of rain.

Noon
The sun is a wounded deer,
That treads pale grass in the skies,
Shaking his golden horns,
Flashing his baleful eyes.

Sunset
The sun is an eagle old,
There in the windless west,
Atop of the spirit-cliffs
He builds him a crimson nest.

VACHEL LINDSAY

ZEBRA

The eagle's shadow runs across the plain,
Towards the distant, nameless, air-blue mountains.
But the shadows of the round young Zebra
Sit close between their delicate hoofs all day, where
they stand immovable,
And wait for the evening, wait to stretch out, blue,
Upon a plain, painted brick-red by the sunset,
And to wander to the water-hole.

ISAK DINESEN

EARTHY ANECDOTE

Every time the bucks went clattering
Over Oklahoma
A firecat bristled in the way.

Wherever they went,
They went clattering,
Until they swerved
In a swift, circular line
To the right,
Because of the firecat.

Or until they swerved
In a swift, circular line
To thc lcft,
Because of the firecat.

The bucks clattered.
The firecat went leaping,
To the right, to the left,
And
Bristled in the way.

Later, the firecat closed his bright eyes
And slept.

WALLACE STEVENS

STORIES FROM KANSAS

Little bunches of
grass pretend they are bushes
that never will bow.
        They bow.

Carelessly the earth
escapes, loping out from the
timid little towns
        toward Colorado.

Which of the horses
we passed yesterday whinnied
all night in my dreams?
        I want that one.

WILLIAM STAFFORD

GRASSROOTS

Grass clutches at the dark dirt with finger holds.
Let it be blue grass, barley, rye or wheat,
Let it be button weed or butter-and-eggs,
Let it be Johnny-jump-ups springing clean blue
streaks.
Grassroots down under put fingers into dark dirt.

CARL SANDBURG

NEBRASKA

There, there is no mountain within miles.
The land, slowly rising toward a distant glory,
Is devoid of ornaments or sudden splendor.
It is a land no tourist travels far to see.

Those who ride through it, hurrying to strong streams
Broken and shot across stones, or running to find
Gay palaces to possess the mind, hardly notice as they
pass,
Or note with anger, the constant, level wind.

Yet this, the one companion of that land,
Might tell them, though they are always hurrying,
And though they hate that hot and wheat-high wind:
This was the bed of forgotten seas; this wheat is
blossoming.

JON SWAN

IMPROVED FARM LAND

Tall timber stood here once
here on a corn belt farm along the Monon.
Here the roots of a half mile of trees
dug their runners deep in the loam
for a grip and a hold against windstorms.
Then the axmen came and the chips flew
to the zing of steel and handle—
the lank railsplitters cut the big ones first,
the beeches and the oaks, then the brush.
Dynamite, wagons and horses took the stumps—
the plows sunk their teeth in—
now it is first-class corn land—improved
property—
and the hogs grunt over the fodder crops.
It would come hard now for this half mile of
improved farm land
along the Monon corn belt,
on a piece of Grand Prairie,
to remember once it had a great singing family of
trees.

CARL SANDBURG

THE FLOWER-FED BUFFALOES

The flower-fed buffaloes of the spring
In the days of long ago,
Ranged where the locomotives sing
And the prairie flowers lie low:—
The tossing, blooming, perfumed grass
Is swept away by the wheat,
Wheels and wheels and wheels spin by
In the spring that still is sweet.
But the flower-fed buffaloes of the spring
Left us, long ago.
They gore no more, they bellow no more,
They trundle around the hills no more:—
With the Blackfeet, lying low,
With the Pawnees, lying low,
Lying low.

VACHEL LINDSAY

BUFFALO DUSK

The buffaloes are gone.
And those who saw the buffaloes are gone.
Those who saw the buffaloes by thousands and
how they pawed the prairie sod into dust
with their hoofs, their great heads down
pawing on in a great pageant of dusk,
Those who saw the buffaloes are gone.
And the buffaloes are gone.

CARL SANDBURG

WEST OF CHICAGO

Beneath these plains
Are the bones
Of small horses.
Invisible in the sunlight
The ghosts of dead Indians
Move over the land;
Searching for the ruined settlements
Seeking their scattered children.

In the quiet, neat towns
At night
The houses and small streets
Disappear in the darkness.
And again in the distance
You can hear
Or think you hear
The bare winds
Moving across the great plains.

JOHN DIMOFF

A SOUND FROM THE EARTH

Somewhere, I think in Dakota,
they found the leg bones—just the
big leg bones—of several hundred
buffalo, in a gravel pit.

Near there, a hole in a cliff
has been hollowed so that
the prevailing wind
thrums a note so low and persistent
that bowls of water placed in that
cave will tremble to foam.

The grandfather of Crazy Horse
lived there, they say, at the last,
and his voice like the thrum of the hills
made winter come as he sang, "Boy,
where was your buffalo medicine?
I say you were not brave enough, Boy,
I say Crazy Horse was too cautious."

Then the sound he cried out for his grandson
made that thin Agency soup that they
put before him tremble. The whole
earthen bowl churned into foam.

WILLIAM STAFFORD

SWALLOWS

The prairie wind blew harder than it could,
Even the spines of cactus trembled back,
I crouched in an arroyo clamping my hands
On my eyes the sand was stinging yellow black.

In a break of the black I let my lashes part,
Looked overhead and saw I was not alone,
I could almost reach through the roar and almost touch
A treadmill of swallows almost holding their own.

THOMAS HORNSBY FERRIL

Tossing Waves and Quiet Dunes

I stand as on some mighty eagle's beak,
Eastward the sea absorbing, viewing, (nothing but sea
and sky,)
The tossing waves, the foam, the ships in the distance,
The wild unrest, the snowy, curling caps—
that inbound urge and urge of waves,
Seeking the shores forever.

WALT WHITMAN

OUT OF THE SEA, EARLY

A bloody
egg yolk. A burnt hole
spreading in a sheet. An en-
raged rose threatening to bloom.
A furnace hatchway opening, roaring.
A globular bladder filling with immense
juice. I start to scream. A red hydrocepha-
lic head is born, teetering on the stump of
its neck. When it separates, it leaks rasp-
berry from the horizon down the wide esca-
lator. The cold blue boiling waves cannot
scour out that band, that broadens, slid-
ing toward me up the wet sand slope. The
fox-hair grows, grows thicker on the
upfloating head. By six o'clock,
diffused to ordinary gold,
it exposes each silk thread and rumple in the carpet.

MAY SWENSON

BEGINNING TO SQUALL

A Buoy like a man in a red sou'wester
is uP to the toP of its Boots in the water
  leaning to warn a Blue Boat

      that, BoBBing and shrugging, is nodding "No,"
        till a strong wave comes and it shivers "Yes."
          The white and the green Boats are
              quiBBling, too.
                What is it they don't want to do?

The Bay goes on Bouncing anchor floats,
their colors tennis and tangerine.
Two ruffled gulls laughing are laughing gulls,
  a finial Pair on the gray Pilings.

      Now the Boats are Buttoning slickers on
        which resemBle little tents.
          The Buoy is jumPing uP and down
            showing a Black Belt stenciled "1."

A yellow Boat's last to lower sail
to wraP like a Bandage around the Boom.
  Blades are sharPening in the water
      that Brightens while the sky goes duller.

MAY SWENSON

STORM TIDE ON MEJIT

The wind's spine is broken,
It blows less,
We perform the wind-taboo.
It grows still, still, still,
Wholly still,
The calm, the calm.
The wind-taboo, *e*,
Makes calm, calm, calm.
The surf, surf, surf,
The surf, surf, surf,
The surf, surf, surf,
Plunges, roars,
Plunges, roars,
Plunges, roars,
It flows up,
The sea covers the beach with foam,
It is full of the finest sand,
Stirring up the ground, stirring up the ground.
It slaps, slaps, slaps,
Slaps, slaps, slaps
On the beach, and roars.

MARSHALL ISLANDS POEM
translated from a Micronesian language
by Augustin Krämer and Willard Trask

HOW EVERYTHING HAPPENS
(Based on a Study of the Wave)

happen.
to
up
stacking
is
something
When nothing is happening

When it happens
something
pulls
back
not
to
happen.

When has happened.
pulling back stacking up
happens

has happened stacks up.
When it something nothing
pulls back while

Then nothing is happening.

happens.
and
forward
pushes
up
stacks
something
Then

MAY SWENSON

WITH KIT, AGE 7, AT THE BEACH

We would climb the highest dune,
from there to gaze and come down:
the ocean was performing;
we contributed our climb.

Waves leapfrogged and came
straight out of the storm.
What should our gaze mean?
Kit waited for me to decide.

Standing on such a hill,
what would you tell your child?
That was an absolute vista.
Those waves raced far, and cold.

"How far could you swim, Daddy,
in such a storm?"
"As far as was needed," I said,
and as I talked, I swam.

WILLIAM STAFFORD

SAND DUNES

Sea waves are green and wet,
But up from where they die
Rise others vaster yet,
And those are brown and dry.

They are the sea made land
To come at the fisher town
And bury in solid sand
The men she could not drown.

She may know cove and cape,
But she does not know mankind
If by any change of shape
She hopes to cut off mind.

Men left her a ship to sink:
They can leave her a hut as well;
And be but more free to think
For the one more cast-off shell.

ROBERT FROST

GERMAN SHEPHERD

He has never heard of tides,
of moon and sun
pulling the water to ebb, to flow.
All that he can know
is to outrun
white foam and waves,
wetting his paws, his muzzle,
playing the game
in the joy of a wetness
He can never name ocean.

MYRA COHN LIVINGSTON

GRUNION

The moon mentions
    The grunion will be running;
    time, she says, to catch them spawning
    silver sand;

    time, she says, to slosh the beach,
    wait for the tide;

    time, she says, to wander the waves,
    spill over, flail,
    reach to the foam,
    watch, wait
    catch
        catch
            catch
                (if you can)

MYRA COHN LIVINGSTON

SEAGULLS

Between the under and the upper blue
All day the seagulls climb and swerve and soar,
Arc intersecting arc, curve over curve.

And you may watch them weaving a long time
And never see their pattern twice the same
And never see their pattern once imperfect.

Take any moment they are in the air—
If you could change them, if you had the power
How would you place them other than they are?

What we have labored all our lives to have
And failed, these birds effortlessly achieve;
Freedom that flows in form and still is free.

ROBERT FRANCIS

DRIFTWOOD

Driftwood marks the shore—
The alphabet of ancients
Writing a last word.

DANIEL SMYTHE

SEAL

See how he dives
From the rocks with a zoom!
See how he darts
Through his watery room
Past crabs and eels
And green seaweed,
Past fluffs of sandy
Minnow feed!
See how he swims
With a swerve and a twist,
A flip of the flipper,
A flick of the wrist!
Quicksilver-quick,
Softer than spray,
Down he plunges
And sweeps away;
Before you can think,
Before you can utter
Words like "Dill pickle"
Or "Apple butter,"
Back up he swims
Past sting-ray and shark,
Out with a zoom,
A whoop, a bark;
Before you can say
Whatever you wish,
He plops at your side
With a mouthful of fish!

WILLIAM JAY SMITH

A CONVERSATION

ROSIE PROBERT: What seas did you see,
Tom Cat, Tom Cat,
In your sailoring days
Long long ago?
What sea beasts were
In the wavery green
When you were my master?

CAPTAIN CAT: I'll tell you the truth.
Seas barking like seals,
Blue seas and green,
Seas covered with eels
And mermen and whales.

ROSIE: What seas did you sail
Old whaler when
On the blubbery waves
Between Frisco and Wales
You were my bosun?

CAPTAIN CAT: As true as I'm here
You landlubber Rosie
You cozy love
My easy as easy
My true sweetheart,
Seas green as a bean
Seas gliding with swans
In the seal-barking moon.

DYLAN THOMAS

WAKING FROM A NAP ON THE BEACH

Sounds like big
rashers of bacon frying.
I look up from where I'm lying
expecting to see stripes

red and white. My eyes drop shut,
stunned by the sun.
Now the foam is flame, the long
troughs charcoal, but

still it chuckles and sizzles, it
burns and burns, it never gets done.
The sea is
fat.

MAY SWENSON

Ayii, Ayii,
The great sea has set me in motion,
Set me adrift,
And I move as a weed in the river.
The arch of sky
And mightiness of storms
Encompasses me,
And I am left
Trembling with joy.

EASTERN ESKIMO SONG

Ice Cakes and the Snow's Crust

Ayii, Ayii,
I walked on the ice of the sea.
Wondering, I heard
The song of the sea
And the great sighing
Of new formed ice.
Go then go!
Strength of soul
Brings health
To the place of feasting.

EASTERN ESKIMO SONG

AN EMPTY THREAT

I stay;
But it isn't as if
There wasn't always Hudson's Bay
And the fur trade,
A small skiff
And a paddle blade.

I can just see my tent pegged,
And me on the floor,
Cross-legged,
And a trapper looking in at the door
With furs to sell.

His name's Joe,
Alias John,
And between what he doesn't know
And won't tell
About where Henry Hudson's gone,
I can't say he's much help;
But we get on.

The seal yelp
On an ice cake.
It's not men by some mistake?
No,
There's not a soul
For a windbreak
Between me and the North Pole—

Except always John-Joe,
My French Indian Esquimaux,
And he's off setting traps—
In one himself perhaps.

Give a headshake
Over so much bay
Thrown away
In snow and mist
That doesn't exist,
I was going to say,
For God, man, or beast's sake,
Yet does perhaps for all three.

Don't ask Joe
What it is to him.
It's sometimes dim
What it is to me,
Unless it be
It's the old captain's dark fate
Who failed to find or force a strait
In its two-thousand-mile coast;
And his crew left him where he failed,
And nothing came of all he sailed.

It's to say, 'You and I'–
To such a ghost–
'You and I
Off here
With the dead race of the Great Auk!'
And, 'Better defeat almost,
If seen clear,
Than life's victories of doubt
That need endless talk-talk
To make them out.'

ROBERT FROST

Glorious it is
to see long-haired winter caribou
Returning to the forests,
While the herd follows the ebb-mark of the sea
With a storm of clattering hooves.
Glorious it is
When wandering time is come.

ALASKAN ESKIMO SONG

IN FUR

They hurt no one. They rove the North.
Owning the wilderness, they're not lost.
They couple in joy; in fear, they run.
Old, their lives move still the same—
all a pattern across the land,
one step, one breath, one. . . .

Winter bundles them close; their fur
bunches together in friendly storms.
Everything cold can teach, they learn.
They stand together. The future comes.

WILLIAM STAFFORD

THE BEAR

1

In late winter
I sometimes glimpse bits of steam
coming up from
some fault in the old snow
and bend close and see it is lung-colored
and put down my nose
and know
the chilly, enduring odor of bear.

2

I take a wolf's rib and whittle
it sharp at both ends
and coil it up
and freeze it in blubber and place it out
on the fairway of the bears.

And when it has vanished
I move out on the bear tracks,
roaming in circles
until I come to the first, tentative, dark
splash on the earth.

And I set out
running, following the splashes

of blood, wandering over the world.
At the cut, gashed resting places
I stop and rest,
at the crawl-marks
where he lay out on his belly
to overpass some stretch of bauchy ice
I lie out
dragging myself forward with bear-knives in my fists.

3

On the third day I begin to starve,
at nightfall I bend down as I knew I would
at a turd sopped in blood,
and hesitate, and pick it up,
and thrust it in my mouth, and gnash it down,
and rise
and go on running.

4

On the seventh day
living by now on bear blood alone,
I can see his upturned carcass far out ahead, a
scraggled, steamy hulk,
the heavy fur ruffling in the wind.

I come up to him
and stare at the narrow-spaced, petty eyes,
the dismayed
face laid back on the shoulder, the nostrils
flared, catching
perhaps the first taint of me as he
died.

I hack a ravine in his thigh, and eat and drink,
and tear him down his whole length
and open him and climb in
and close him up after me, against the wind,
and sleep.

5

And dream
of lumbering flatfooted
over the tundra,
stabbed twice from within,
splattering a trail behind me,
splattering it out no matter which way I lurch,
no matter which parabola of bear-transcendence,
which dance of solitude I attempt,
which gravity-clutched leap,
which trudge, which groan.

6

Until one day I totter and fall—
fall on this
stomach that has tried so hard to keep up,
to digest the blood as it leaked in,
to break up
and digest the bone itself: and now the breeze
blows over me, blows off
the hideous belches of ill-digested bear blood
and rotted stomach
and the ordinary, wretched odor of bear,

blows across
my sore, lolled tongue a song
or screech, until I think I must rise up
and dance. And I lie still.

7

I awaken I think. Marshlights
reappear, geese
come trailing again up the flyway.
In her ravine under the old snow the dam-bear
lies, licking
lumps of smeared fur
and drizzly eyes into shapes
with her tongue. And one
hairy-soled trudge stuck out before me,
the next groaned out,
the next,
the next,
the rest of my days I spend
wandering, wondering
what, anyway,
was that sticky infusion, that rank flavor of blood, that
    poetry, by which I lived?

GALWAY KINNELL

TO CHRIST OUR LORD

The legs of the elk punctured the snow's crust
And wolves floated lightfooted on the land
Hunting Christmas elk living and frozen.
Indoors snow melted in a basin and a woman basted
A bird spread over coals by its wings and head.

Snow had sealed the windows; candles lit
The Christmas meal. The special grace chilled
The cooked bird, being long-winded and the room cold.
During the words a boy thought, is it fitting
To eat this creature killed on the wing?

For he had shot it himself, climbing out
Alone on snowshoes in the Christmas dawn,
The fallen snow swirling and the snowfall gone,
Heard its throat scream and the rifle shouted,
Watched it drop, and fished from the snow the dead.

He had not wanted to shoot. The sound
Of wings beating into the hushed morning
Had stirred his love, and the things
In his gloves froze, and he wondered
Famishing, could he fire? Then he fired.

Now the grace praised his wicked act. At its end
The bird on the plate
Stared at his stricken appetite.
There had been nothing to do but surrender,
To kill and to eat; he ate as he had killed, with wonder.

At night on snowshoes on the drifting field
He wondered again, for whom had love stirred?
The stars glittered on the snow and nothing answered.
Than the Swan spread her wings, cross of the cold north,
The pattern and mirror of the acts of earth.

GALWAY KINNELL

We will watch the Northern Lights
playing their game of ball
in the cold, glistening country.
Then we will sit in beauty on the mountain
and watch the small stars
in their sleepless flight.

ABANAKI INDIAN SONG

THE VIEW FROM HERE

In Antarctica drooping their little shoulders
like bottles the penguins stand, small,
sad, black—and the wind
bites hard over them.

Edging that continent they huddle to turn their eyes.
Penguins, we can't help you; and all that cold
hangs over us too, wide beyond thought.
We too stand and wait.

WILLIAM STAFFORD

When Spring came,
Leaves grew with a green fresh
feeling,
And the warmth of the sun
Was beginning to be felt,
And the Animals of the Earth
Awoke, breathing the fresh new
smell.
Of life all over again.

It's like the wind,
Gently blowing,
Making love to everything
Before it moves on
Yet returning.

TLINGLIT INDIAN SONG

ESKIMO CHANT

There is joy in
Feeling the warmth
Come to the great world
And seeing the sun
Follow its old footprints
In the summer night.

There is fear in
Feeling the cold
Come to the great world
And seeing the moon
—Now new moon, now full moon—
Follow its old footprints
In the winter night.

translated by Knud Rasmussen

Across Open Fields

THE WAKING

I strolled across
An open field;
The sun was out;
Heat was happy.

This way! This way!
The wren's throat shimmered,
Either to other,
The blossoms sang.

The stones sang,
The little ones did,
And flowers jumped
Like small goats.

A ragged fringe
Of daisies waved;
I wasn't alone
In a grove of apples.

Far in the wood
A nestling sighed;
The dew loosened
Its morning smells.

I came where the river
Ran over stones:
My ears knew
An early joy.

And all the waters
Of all the streams
Sang in my veins
That summer day.

THEODORE ROETHKE

CROWS

I like to walk
And hear the black crows talk.

I like to lie
And watch crows sail the sky.

I like the crow
That wants the wind to blow:

I like the one
That thinks the wind is fun.

I like to see
Crows spilling from a tree,

And try to find
The top crow left behind.

I like to hear
Crows caw that spring is near.

I like the great
Wild clamor of crow hate

Three farms away
When owls are out by day.

I like the slow
Tired homeward-flying crow;

I like the sight
Of crows for my good night.

DAVID McCORD

APRIL

The little goat
crops
new grass lying down
leaps up eight inches
into air and
lands on four feet.
Not a tremor—
solid in the
spring and serious
he walks away.

YVOR WINTERS

BLUE-BUTTERFLY DAY

It is blue-butterfly day here in spring,
And with these sky-flakes down in flurry on flurry
There is more unmixed color on the wing
Than flowers will show for days unless they hurry.

But these are flowers that fly and all but sing:
And now from having ridden out desire
They lie closed over in the wind and cling
Where wheels have freshly sliced the April mire.

ROBERT FROST

MAY 10TH

I mean
the fiddleheads have forced their babies,
blind topknots first, up from the thinking rhizomes
and the shrew's children, twenty to a teaspoon,
breathe to their own astonishment
in the peephole burrow.

I mean
a new bat hangs upside down in the privy;
its eyes are stuck tight, its wrinkled mouth twitches
and in the pond, itself an invented puddle,
tadpoles quake from the jello
and come into being.

I mean, walk softly.
The maple's little used-up bells are dropping
and the new leaves are now unpacking,
still wearing their dime-store lacquer,
still cramped and wet from the journey.

MAXINE KUMIN

THE BREATHING

An absolute
patience.
Trees stand
up to their knees in
fog. The fog
slowly flows
uphill.
          White
cobwebs, the grass
leaning where deer
have looked for apples.
The woods
from brook to where
the top of the hill looks
over the fog, send up
not one bird.
So absolute, it is
no other than
happiness itself, a breathing
too quiet to hear.

DENISE LEVERTOV

CICADA

I lay with my heart under me,
under the white sun,
face down to fields
and a life that gleamed
under my palm like an emerald hinge.
I sheltered him where we lay alive
under the body of the sun.
Trees there dropped their shadows
like black fruit,
and the thin-necked sparrows came
crying through the light.

At my life line I felt
his bent, bright knee
work like a latch.
He was safe with me
in the room my round bones made–
or might have been–
but he sang like a driven nail
and his skinless eyes looked out,
wanting himself as he was.

Wisdom was imprecise,
my hand's loose judgment dark.
Some jewel work straining in his thigh
broke like a kingdom.
I let him go,
a jackstraw limping to the dynamo
of hunger under the hungering sun
and the world's quick gizzard.
High noon hummed,
all parts in place–
or nearly so.

ADRIEN STOUTENBURG

BATS

A bat is born
Naked and blind and pale.
His mother makes a pocket of her tail
And catches him. He clings to her long fur
By his thumbs and toes and teeth.
And then the mother dances through the night
Doubling and looping, soaring, somersaulting—
Her baby hangs on underneath.
All night, in happiness, she hunts and flies.
Her high sharp cries
Like shining needlepoints of sound
Go out into the night and, echoing back,
Tell her what they have touched.
She hears how far it is, how big it is,
Which way it's going:
She lives by hearing.
The mother eats the moths and gnats she catches
In full flight; in full flight
The mother drinks the water of the pond
She skims across. Her baby hangs on tight.
Her baby drinks the milk she makes him
In moonlight or starlight, in mid-air.
Their single shadow, printed on the moon
Or fluttering across the stars,
Whirls on all night; at daybreak

The tired mother flaps home to her rafter.
The others all are there.
They hang themselves up by their toes,
They wrap themselves in their brown wings.
Bunched upside-down, they sleep in air.
Their sharp ears, their sharp teeth, their quick sharp
faces
Are dull and slow and mild.
All the bright day, as the mother sleeps,
She folds her wings about her sleeping child.

RANDALL JARRELL

THE HERMIT PICKS BERRIES

At midday the birds doze.
So does he.

The frogs cover themselves.
So does he.

The breeze holds its breath in the poplars.
Not one leaf turns its back.
He admires the stillness.

The snake uncoils its clay self
in the sun on a rock in the pasture.
It is the hermit's pasture.
He encourages the snake.

At this hour a goodly number
of blueberries decide to ripen.
Once they were wax white.
Then came the green of small bruises.
After that, the red of bad welts.
All this time they enlarged themselves.
Now they are true blue.

The hermit whistles as he picks.
Later he will put on his shirt
and walk to town for some cream.

MAXINE KUMIN

BULLFROG

With their lithe, long, strong legs,
Some frogs are able
To thump upon double-
Bass strings, though pond water deadens and clogs.

But you, bullfrog, you pump out
Whole fogs full of horn—a threat
As of a liner looming. True
That, first hearing you
Disgorging your gouts of darkness like a wounded
god,
Not utterly fantastically, I expected
(As in some antique tale depicted)
A broken-down bull up to its belly in mud,
Sucking black swamp up, belching out black cloud

And a squall of gudgeon and lilies.
A surprise
Now, to see you, a boy's prize,
No bigger than a rat, with all dumb silence
In your little old woman hands.

TED HUGHES

SNAKE

I saw a young snake glide
Out of the mottled shade
And hang, limp on a stone:
A thin mouth, and a tongue
Stayed, in the still air.

It turned; it drew away;
Its shadow bent in half;
It quickened, and was gone.

I felt my slow blood warm.
I longed to be that thing,
The pure, sensuous form.

And I may be, some time.

THEODORE ROETHKE

IN FIELDS OF SUMMER

The sun rises,
The goldenrod blooms,
I drift in fields of summer,
My life is adrift in my body,
It shines in my heart and hands, in my teeth,
It shines up at the old crane
Who holds out his drainpipe of a neck
And creaks along in the blue,

And the goldenrod shines with its life, too,
And the grass, look,
The great field wavers and flakes,
The rumble of bumblebees keeps deepening,
A phoebe flutters up,
A lark bursts up all dew.

GALWAY KINNELL

THE MOCKINGBIRD

Look one way and the sun is going down,
Look the other and the moon is rising.
The sparrow's shadow's longer than the lawn.
The bats squeak, "Night is here;" the birds cheep,
    "Day is gone."
On the willow's highest branch, monopolizing
Day and night, cheeping, squeaking, soaring,
The mockingbird is imitating life.

All day the mockingbird has owned the yard.
As light first woke the world, the sparrows trooped
Onto the seedy lawn; the mockingbird
Chased them off shrieking. Hour by hour, fighting hard
To make the world his own, he swooped
On thrushes, thrashers, jays, and chickadees—
At noon he drove away a big black cat.

Now, in the moonlight, he sits here and sings.
A thrush is singing, then a thrasher, then a jay—
Then, all at once, a cat begins meowing.
A mockingbird can sound like anything.
He imitates the world he drove away
So well that, for a minute, in the moonlight,
Which one's the mockingbird? Which one's the world?

RANDALL JARRELL

MOLES

Every day that their sky droops down,
They shrug before it can harden
and root for life, rumpling along
toward the green part of the garden.

Every day the moles' dirt sky
sags upon their shoulders,
and mine too sags on many a day,
pinned by heavy boulders.

We get tired, the moles and I,
toiling down our burrows.
They shrug dirt along their way,
And I rumple on through sorrows.

WILLIAM STAFFORD

RIDING IN THE RAIN

This is the way we come
in a jingle of bits and chains
and the pocking of shoes on stone
down pasture, across bluff

old gelding, older mare
where a sweet unhurried rain
has lacquered every leaf
and the trees are chocolate bars.

The good mud underfoot
opens its matted fur
to pop up snails for pearls,
then licks itself like a cat.

Two dozen orange newts
shimmy on granite boulders
like smalltown belly dancers.
The ferns breathe cinnamon.

The horses steam out dander.
They blow their noses in
a tunnel of birch and popple.
Their droppings multiply,
a cluster of old yellow apples.

This is the way we come,
old gelding, older mare
in easy spattered air
like lazy mastodons
going from here to there.

MAXINE KUMIN

THE HERON

The heron stands in water where the swamp
Has deepened to the blackness of a pool,
Or balances with one leg on a hump
Of marsh grass heaped above a musk-rat hole.

He walks the shallow with an antic grace.
The great feet break the ridges of the sand,
The long eye notes the minnow's hiding place.
His beak is quicker than a human hand.

He jerks a frog across his bony lip,
Then points his heavy bill above the wood.
The wide wings flap but once to lift him up.
A single ripple starts from where he stood.

THEODORE ROETHKE

In the swamp in secluded recesses,
A shy and hidden bird is warbling a song.

Solitary the thrush,
The hermit withdrawn to himself, avoiding the
settlements,
Sings by himself a song.

WALT WHITMAN

3

Sometimes I see them,
The South-going Canada geese,
At evening, coming down
In pink light, over the pond, in great,
Loose, always dissolving V's—
I go out into the field,
Amazed and moved, and listen
To the cold, lonely yelping
Of those tranced bodies in the sky,
Until I feel on the point
Of breaking to a sacred, bloodier speech.

GALWAY KINNELL

LATE AT NIGHT

Falling separate into the dark
the hailstone yelps of geese pattered
through our roof; startled we listened.

Those V's of direction swept by unseen
so orderly that we paused. But then
faltering back through their circle they came.

Were they lost up there in the night?
They always knew the way, we thought.
You looked at me across the room:—

We live in a terrible season.

WILLIAM STAFFORD

HALF MOON

The moon goes over the water.
How tranquil the sky is!
She goes scything slowly
the old shimmer from the river;
meanwhile a young frog
takes her for a little mirror.

FEDERICO GARCÍA LORCA
translated by W. S. Merwin

MILL VALLEY

Out with the mountain moon, stinging clear,
Crept through a footpath, old raccoon,
Gray in her coat, a ragged ear
Perked to the silence.
Old raccoon with her furrowed frown,
Gloved, dressed in her evening gown,
Crept near the windowpane, to feast.

MYRA COHN LIVINGSTON

THE PRESENCE

Something went crabwise
across the snow this morning.
Something went hard and slow
over our hayfield.
It could have been a raccoon
lugging a knapsack,
it could have been a porcupine
carrying a tennis racket,
it could have been something
supple as a red fox
dragging the squawk and spatter
of a crippled woodcock.
Ten knuckles underground
those bones are seeds now
pure as baby teeth
lined up in the burrow.
I cross on snowshoes
cunningly woven from
the skin and sinews of
something else that went before.

MAXINE KUMIN

MARCH 8, 1840

In the brooks the slight grating sound of small cakes of ice,
floating with various speed, is full of content and promise,
and where the water gurgles under a natural bridge,
you may hear these hasty rafts hold conversation in an undertone.
Every rill is a channel for the juices of a meadow.
Last year's grasses and flower-stalks have been steeped in rain and snow,
and now the brooks flow with meadow tea. . . .

HENRY DAVID THOREAU

THE OLD WALKING SONG

The Road goes ever on and on
  Down from the door where it began.
Now far ahead the Road has gone,
  And I must follow, if I can,
Pursuing it with eager feet,
  Until it joins some larger way
Where many paths and errands meet.
  And whither then? I cannot say.

J. R. R. TOLKIEN

Someone Small but a Piece of It All

WHO AM I?

The trees ask me,
And the sky,
And the sea asks me
Who am I?

The grass asks me,
And the sand,
And the rocks ask me
Who am I?

The wind tells me
At nightfall,
And the rain tells me
Someone small.

Someone small
Someone small
But a piece
of
it
all.

FELICE HOLMAN

from

SONG OF THE OPEN ROAD

Afoot and light-hearted I take to the open road,
Healthy, free, the world before me,
The long brown path before me leading wherever I
choose.

Henceforth I ask not good-fortune, I myself am
good-fortune,
Henceforth I whimper no more, postpone no more,
need nothing,
Done with indoor complaints, libraries, querulous
criticisms,
Strong and content I travel the open road.

WALT WHITMAN

THERE WAS A CHILD WENT FORTH

There was a child went forth every day,
And the first object he look'd upon, that object he
became,
And that object became part of him for the day or a
certain part of the day,
Or for many years or stretching cycles of years.

The early lilacs became part of this child,
And grass and white and red morning-glories, and
white and red clover, and the song of the
phoebe-bird,
And the Third-month lambs and the sow's pink-faint
litter, and the mare's foal and the cow's calf,
And the noisy brood of the barnyard or by the mire of
the pond-side,
And the fish suspending themselves so curiously below
there, and the beautiful curious liquid,
And the water-plants with their graceful flat heads, all
became part of him.

WALT WHITMAN

LISTENING

My father could hear a little animal step,
or a moth in the dark against the screen,
and every far sound called the listening out
into places where the rest of us had never been.

More spoke to him from the soft wild night
than came to our porch for us on the wind;
we would watch him look up and his face go keen
till the walls of the world flared, widened.

My father heard so much that we still stand
inviting the quiet by turning the face,
waiting for a time when something in the night
will touch us too from that other place.

WILLIAM STAFFORD

FATHER'S VOICE

"No need to get home early;
the car can see in the dark."
He wanted me to be rich
the only way we could,
easy with what we had.

And always that was his gift,
given for me ever since,
easy gift, a wind
that keeps on blowing for flowers
or birds wherever I look.

World, I am your slow guest,
one of the common things
that move in the sun and have
close, reliable friends
in the earth, in the air, in the rock.

WILLIAM STAFFORD

THE HERMIT

I dwell apart
From the world of men.

I lift my eyes
To the mighty hills,
And sit in silent reverie
By rushing streams.
My songs
Are the whisperings of the winds
And the soft murmurs
Of falling rain.

Blossoms open
And flutter to earth again.
Men come
And men go;
Year follows year,
And life goes on.

HSÜ PÊN

A LIVING

A man should never earn his living,
if he earns his life he'll be lovely.

A bird
picks up its seeds or little snails
between heedless earth and heaven
in heedlessness.

But, the plucky little sport, it gives to life
song, and chirruping, gay feathers, fluff-shadowed
warmth
and all the unspeakable charm of bird hopping and
fluttering and being birds.
—And we, we get it all from them for nothing.

D. H. LAWRENCE

I have not so much emulated the birds that musically
sing,
I have abandon'd myself to flights, broad circles.
The hawk, the seagull, have far more possess'd me than
the canary or mocking-bird,
I have not felt to warble and trill, however sweetly,
I have felt to soar in freedom and in the fullness of
power, joy, volition.

WALT WHITMAN

I am weary of these times and their dull burden,
  Sweating and laboring in the summer noontide,
And the hot stench of inland forges
  Sickens my nostrils.

Soon there will be no more metals to plunder,
  There will be no more forests to slash and
    dismember,
Then, O chosen people, nation of fortune,
  Where is thy glory?

LUCIUS BEEBE

HARD QUESTIONS

Why not mark out the land
into neat rectangles
squares and clover leafs?

Put on them cubes of
varying sizes
according to use–
dwellings
    singles/multiples
complexes
    commercial/industrial.

Bale them together with
bands of roads.

What if a child shall cry
"I have never known spring!
I have never seen autumn!"

What if a man shall say
"I have never heard
silence fraught with living as
in swamp or forest!"
What if the eye shall never see
marsh bird and muskrats?

Does not the heart need
wildness?
Does not the thought need
something
to rest upon
not self-made by man,
a bosom
not his own?

MARGARET TSUDA

We need the tonic of wildness,
to wade sometimes in the marshes
where the bittern and the meadow-hen lurk,
and hear the booming of the snipe;
to smell the whispering sedge
where only some wilder and more solitary fowl builds
her nest,
and the mink crawls on its belly close to the ground.

HENRY DAVID THOREAU

TO LOOK AT ANY THING

To look at any thing,
If you would know that thing,
You must look at it long:
To look at this green and say
'I have seen spring in these
Woods,' will not do—you must
Be the thing you see:
You must be the dark snakes of
Stems and ferny plumes of leaves,
You must enter in
To the small silences between
The leaves,
You must take your time
And touch the very peace
They issue from.

JOHN MOFFITT

I READ A TIGHT-FISTED POEM ONCE

I touched the nothingness of air once and felt nothing. I touched it again and felt a breeze.

I filled my lungs with air and smelled nothing. I filled my body and soul with it and smelled the violets.

I read a tight-fisted poem once and realized nothing. I read it again and was surprised to see it burst into blossom and reveal its inner palm.

To look once is to be blind. To look again is to see inside.

To run quickly and glance is to realize nothing. To move slowly and become what you look at is to realize that nothing does not exist.

Do you see what it really is or do you see what you want it to be?

Is he saying what is in his heart or is he saying what he thinks is in yours?

To see a person is to know what he is.

To see through a person is to know why he is like that.

To know what a forest is you must walk in that forest and become a part of the green coolness that is the forest.

And when you return they will say, "Where have you been?"

And you will reply, "I have been a forest." And they will look at you and sigh, and wonder when you will learn that you can't go around pretending to be what you aren't.

And you will know what they are thinking and you will say, "Ah! But how will I know how a forest feels unless I feel it, too?" And they will wonder when their problem child is going to change and begin to learn something useful.

NANCY WOODS

FOR POETS

Stay beautiful
but dont stay down underground too long
Dont turn into a mole
or a worm
or a root
or a stone

Come on out into the sunlight
Breathe in trees
Knock out mountains
Commune with snakes
& be the very hero of birds

Dont forget to poke your head up
& blink
think
Walk all around
Swim upstream

Dont forget to fly

AL YOUNG

Indexes

INDEX OF POEMS AND POETS

INDEX OF FIRST LINES

ABOUT THE EDITOR

Nancy Larrick has become known in recent years for poetry anthologies which speak directly to young people today—about the things they are interested in and using the language they know. For each book, selections have been made with the help of young people, who insist upon poems that "tell it like it is" and reject those they call "too sweet."

On City Streets, first published in 1968, is a collection of poems and photographs that capture the heart of the city. It was followed by *I Heard a Scream in the Street*. Nancy Larrick's third book of poems and photographs, *Room for Me and a Mountain Lion*, includes over one hundred poems of open space, selected with the help of young readers who revel in what Whitman called "eating and sleeping with the earth."

Nancy Larrick grew up in Winchester, Virginia, and, from childhood, explored the fields and orchards of her father's farm in the Shenandoah Valley, as well as the slopes and ravines of the Blue Ridge Mountains nearby.

After graduating from Goucher College, she became a classroom teacher, then an editor and writer. She received her master's degree in English literature at Columbia University and her doctorate at New York University. She is currently director of the Poetry Workshop at Lehigh University where she is adjunct professor of education. To millions of parents, she is known as the author of *A Parent's Guide to Children's Reading*, often referred to as a classic in its field.

Nancy Larrick and her husband, Alexander L. Crosby, live in an old stone farm house on fifty wooded acres in Bucks County, Pennsylvania.